S0-BAH-326

WILDERNESS SURVIVAL GUIDE FOR KIDS

How to Build a Fire, Perform First Aid, Build Shelter, Forage for Food, Find Water, and Everything Else You Need to Know to Survive in the Outdoors

Rick Bayne

ISBN: 978-1-957590-24-0

For questions, email: Support@AwesomeReads.org

Please consider writing a review!

Just visit: AwesomeReads.org/review

Copyright 2022. Canyon Press. All Rights Reserved.

No part of this book may be reproduced or transmitted in any form or by any means, electronic or mechanical, including photocopying, recording, or by any other form without written permission from the publisher.

FREE BONUS

SCAN TO GET OUR NEXT
BOOK FOR FREE!

TABLE OF CONTENTS

INTRODUCTION:

WHAT CAN YOU EXPECT FROM THIS BOOK?

This book is full of survival skills that will help you throughout your life. Sometimes, we get into situations that scare us or dangerous things happen that can hurt us if we don't know what to do. Being prepared is a skill that can be useful for a lifetime. This book will teach you how to be your own superhero and show you that you can do what it takes to protect yourself and others when an emergency happens. Whether you're separated from a parent at a crowded mall or you find yourself lost in the wilderness, this guide will explain how to stay calm and take control of the situation.

This book is laid out in an easy-to-read format. The skills in each lesson will give you confidence and peace of mind, knowing you will be able to overcome any situation. It's best to practice these skills in a safe place with your parents or caregivers. Testing the skills you learn in this book will help you understand the core concepts to the best of your ability. You can do this!

Staying Calm

As we dive into learning about survival, the most important skill you can master is the art of staying calm. Staying calm allows you to switch from panic mode to a solution-focused mindset. Without the ability to remain calm in high-pressure situations, you will not be able to properly apply any of these new survival skills. Practicing these skills ahead of time is the perfect way to make sure that you'll remember to breathe during an otherwise scary situation and take the time to analyze the situation calmly. An easy way to help yourself remember what to do in a dangerous situation is to learn the acronym S.T.O.P., which stands for Stop, Think, Observe, and Plan.

Being Prepared Starts With Planning

The best way to prepare for unexpected situations is to expect the unexpected. If you're planning a day out in large, crowded areas, talk with your parent or guardian and plan for specific things that might happen throughout your day. If you are going with your family on a camping trip or out for a hike, be sure to pack basic necessities that you may need in case you are separated from the group. Be sure you know how to use items such as a compass, matches, lighters, and other materials before you need them.

SECTION 1:

GENERAL KNOWLEDGE

The city can be a scary place, especially if you're not familiar with it or don't get to visit very often. This first section will teach you the survival skills in an urban environment. Here are some things that you should have with you and keep in mind if you're out in the city with your family and you find yourself in an emergency:

- Cell phone: If your parents or guardians don't allow you to carry a personal cell phone yet, that's okay. Try to stay near someone with a phone at all times. Whether it is a friend, older sibling, or caregiver, keep close so that if an emergency happens, you have a way to contact someone.

- Water: Staying hydrated is really important. If you become dehydrated, your body will start acting funny. When you are out and about in the city, you'll want to make sure you feel your best

4

so that you are prepared and ready for the day no matter what happens.

- Know your meeting place: Tell your parents or guardians you need a safety meeting before going out into the city. They will be so impressed that you took the initiative to keep yourself safe. Look at a local map of the city, and decide on a specific place to meet if you become separated. Talk about it and then try to drive or walk by the place so that everyone is familiar with it.

- Know the street name of your meeting place: It can be hard, but try to remember the name of the street for your meeting place. This will help you communicate where you need to go to another adult who might be helping you if you get lost.

- Know an emergency phone number: Memorize a number that you can call in the event of an emergency to get in touch with your parents or guardians. Knowing this information is the easiest way to find them, and it's the best way to help other adults understand what you need.

- Remember what others in your group are wearing: Take a moment to take a mental picture before you go out for the day. This means just taking time to notice little things (i.e., *Mom is wearing a pink shirt*). This will help you look for those colors in crowds and help you find your parents faster.

CHAPTER 1:

SITUATIONAL AWARENESS

Survival might sound like a scary word. Sometimes when we think of survival, we imagine bad things happening. However, that isn't always the case. The best way to think about survival skills is to think of them as tools that help you be prepared just in case something bad does happen. When it comes to survival skills, you have to think smart and practice.

The very first survival skill we will teach you is called situational awareness. Situational awareness means that you take time to be observant and notice things about your surroundings. You may notice street names and remember them as you take a walk, or you may notice how many people are in the room. You may even notice that you can hear certain sounds. All these things are ways that you can be situationally aware. We will give you some examples of how to use situational awareness to help you through a possible scary situation. Before we dive into what it takes to have great situational awareness, let's explore the three stages of situational awareness.

Stage 1: Perceiving

The first level of situational awareness is perceiving. This is a big word, but it simply means seeing or noticing what is going on around you. Did you know that you have a secret superpower? You do! Kids are naturally curious. This is the perfect time to use that curiosity to explore and remember your surroundings. Keep yourself safe by exploring. Make it a game to see if you can notice patterns, shapes, colors, or even things that start with the same letter. Paying attention to your surroundings doesn't have to be boring.

But during your exploration, remember to look around and make sure you're not walking away from your parents or guardians. Sometimes, we become so interested in something that we forget to pay attention to everything else that's going on around us.

Stage 2: Understanding

As you become a big kid, you learn what is and what isn't dangerous. You learn not to cross the street without looking both ways, and you learn to make sure you have floats in the pool if you can't swim. But we don't always understand that a situation is dangerous until we're already in trouble. Talk to your parents every time you travel and discuss possible dangers. For example, if you are visiting the beach, you could discuss what dangers you may encounter there, such as riptides, jellyfish, and mean people. Knowing what *could* happen is the best way to avoid danger if you can.

Stage 3: Predicting

The last stage is kind of like magic. You get to predict what you think will happen. It's like looking into a crystal ball. You take what you've seen in your surroundings and add it to what you understand before deciding what you think you should do. Is it safe? Do you feel comfortable? The last stage of anything usually means a final decision, and that is exactly the case here. Once you've noticed something and you understand what it is or why it's happening, then you have to decide what action to take next.

For example, you noticed a car is coming your way at a fast speed. You need to cross the street, but you know that you won't be able to cross the street before the car gets to you. You decide to wait for the car to pass by. Congratulations! You used your situational awareness to avoid getting hurt. Once you've learned to use all three of these skills anywhere you go, you can call yourself a situational master!

Learning to Be Observant

We're not all good at being observant, but if we practice it at an earlier age, then it can become something that is second nature. There are many ways to learn how to become more observant. Start by talking with your parents or caregivers about what it means to be observant. This can help you pinpoint little ways you can start to become more observant every day. Did you know that being observant can be fun? You can turn observational skills into a game or use them when you clean your room.

1. **Word-search activity books:** These types of books are so much fun and can help you build those observational skills. Taking time to find each word in a jumble of letters may just seem like fun, but it's actually teaching you to pick out something familiar to you in the midst of a crowd of other things.

2. **Learn how to organize and put things away:** When you see that something isn't where it belongs, go put the item in the correct place. Not only does this help you notice when something is out of place, but it also improves your organizational skills. Chores or challenges? It's not always fun to have to put things away or tidy up, but when you think about how it can help you stay safe, it can make the task easier.

3. **Play Games Like "I Spy":** Who doesn't love a good game? Every kid loves games, and playing a game like "I Spy" is very beneficial to you. It teaches you to notice little details about things. You can play by yourself or with friends or family.

Signs of Danger

The thought of being in danger can be scary. We may want to run away and hide under the bed, but becoming a big kid means learning what to do in a dangerous situation so that you can avoid it was much as possible. If you can't avoid danger, you should learn how to protect yourself and make the best choices. Unfortunately, danger can be anywhere. This is why learning how to use survival skills is so important. Learning how to spot signs of danger comes with practice, experience, and being observant. Here are some key dangers that you should recognize in order to practice better awareness:

1. **Traffic:** This is a basic but crucial lesson to learn. Work with the adults in your life to understand the importance of being mindful of vehicles and looking both ways. At times, even adults have trouble with traffic. Learning to be aware of traffic at all times when walking on the sidewalk or crossing the street can prepare you to stay safe now and in the future.

2. **Animals running away from an area:** If you see an animal running toward you or away from the direction you are going, that should be a big hint to pay attention. Animals tend to sense danger before we do. If you see groups of birds, deer, or other animals hurriedly leaving an area, it could be a sign of danger. Animals will run away from people, but they could also be running away from rockslides, earthquakes, or fires.

3. **People leaving an area:** Seeing a large mass of people suddenly leaving an area is rarely a good sign. Unless they are at Disney World and the Mickey Mouse Parade is about to start, then it's safe to say that you shouldn't continue in the direction that other people are leaving without understanding why.

4. **Bad weather:** Whether lost in the woods or separated from your parents in the city, it's always a good idea to seek shelter if dark clouds start rolling in and thunder is rumbling. Make sure you know how to recognize various weather situations such as thunderstorms, tornados, hurricanes, hail storms, lightning, and more.

5. **Suspicious people and strangers:** When it comes to your safety, remember not to talk to strangers. This is very important. If lost by yourself, it's better to trust no one than to risk trusting the wrong person. You need to be wary of other people acting strangely or suspiciously by doing things like:

- Dressing in very strange clothes
- Staring at you
- Following you for extended periods of time
- Following you very closely
- "Extra" nice people who offer you things
- Touching
- Pointing

6. **Distressing sounds:** If you hear someone screaming, then you should immediately move away from the screaming or any other distressing sound.

Avoid Distractions

Adults know how easy it is to get distracted, but it can be even worse for kids. You're still exploring the world with a more curious mindset than adults do. With that curiosity comes the challenge of being easily distracted, which can lead to you getting lost, hurt, or worse. Technology makes this challenge harder than ever with such easy access to games, shows, social media, and various other fun apps on our phones. The important thing here is that you let your parents help you learn to focus your attention on the task at hand and not allow your mind to wander. Here are some ways your parents can help you learn to focus and not get distracted so easily:

1. **Don't watch TV or play with your phone while eating:** This simple step can help you become comfortable with paying attention to what you're doing instead of watching something else at the same time. Whether it's walking somewhere or just eating, it's better to focus on one thing at a time.

2. **Limit access to technology:** A great way to solve problems with attention is to avoid distractions altogether. Put your phone and video games away at a particular time of day, such as when you're doing your daily chores.

3. **Encourage alternate sources of entertainment**: Your parents or caregivers should encourage

you to engage with a variety of fun things such as art, sports, music, or simply going outside to play. The adults in your life should show you that you don't have to stare at a screen every single hour.

Here are some ways that distractions can be a danger to you:

1. **You could get lost:** You could be walking and staring at your phone, which may cause you to lose sight of where you're going. Basically, you could lose your parents or get lost somewhere because you were distracted instead of watching where you were going.

2. **You could get hurt:** You could be looking at someone doing something funny on the sidewalk or staring at your phone, and you might end up walking into the road without looking for traffic.

3. **You could miss a sign of danger:** If something has completely distracted you, then you will be much less wary of potential signs of danger that are around you, such as suspicious strangers or an aggressive wild animal. Remember that warnings and sounds of distress can't be heard over loud headphones.

Staying In Well-Lit Areas

For multiple reasons, especially if you are lost or alone, you should always try to stay in well-lit areas for your own safety. Things that wouldn't be a danger in the light can be dangerous in the dark. Children often have a natural tendency to stay away from dark areas, but sometimes curiosity wins you over. Here are a few of those dangers that you should know about:

1. **Bad people:** This doesn't apply to everyone who might decide to chill out in the dark, but if someone does have bad intentions, then they will likely choose to act from a darker area where they can't be seen.

2. **Dangerous insects or animals:** Most dangerous insects, animals, and reptiles prefer hunting in the dark where they can't be seen.

3. **Potholes and obstacles:** Even the simplest things, such as walking in an open field, can be dangerous if it's completely dark. There could be holes in the ground that cause you to fall and get hurt.

So, we now know of a few dangers that could lurk anywhere in the darkness, but what are some typical dark areas all children should avoid?

- Alleyways
- Parking lots
- Under bridges
- Parks
- Beaches
- Abandoned buildings
- Closed gas stations

Where to Go in Crowds

When in a very populated area, the fast pace and crowds can be overwhelming for children and even adults. Feeling over-whelmed in a large crowd is a scary possibility, but with a few protocols and plans in place, this situation can be managed. Here are some ways for you to make safer choices in large crowds if you get lost or separated from your group:

1. **Have a designated meeting spot:** While traveling with your family, take a moment to choose a designated meeting spot in the event you become separated from them. It should be something that stands out and can be easily spotted. For example, if you're at the mall, decide beforehand you'll meet at the play area if you get separated. Play areas are centrally

located, cover a wide area, and are typically bright and colorful, which allows them to be seen from a distance.

2. **Avoid large crowds when possible:** Learning to navigate through large crowds is an important skill. However, an equally important skill is learning to avoid getting caught in the middle of a large crowd in the first place. In busy areas, staying on the outside of the group can help you avoid getting caught up in the middle.

3. **Take it slow:** When in cities and large crowds, it can be easy to get caught up in the fast pace of things and start walking too fast. Hold an adult's hand if necessary, and navigate through the crowds at a pace that is more suitable for you. Walking slower and more carefully will ensure you aren't separated from your group.

Now that you know more about situational awareness, you'll be ready to safely manage a variety of life situations because you'll encounter them with a more prepared mindset. Teaching yourself to be observant will ensure that you pay attention to your environment and try to predict any changes that may occur around you. While exploring, you'll be more aware of any signs of danger, and you can pay more attention by avoiding distractions.

Whether you are lost or simply out and about, you'll be more mindful about staying in well-lit areas and know how to navigate through large crowds. This is what situational awareness looks like. When you master the skill of situational awareness, you will be able to avoid or safely manage whatever dangerous situations you might encounter.

CHAPTER 2:

WHAT TO DO WHEN SEPARATED FROM YOUR PARENT OR GUARDIAN

If you utilize situational awareness, more times than not you will find yourself in a more favorable situation. But sometimes, even when we do everything perfectly, things still don't work out as we hoped. In some instances, you may find yourself separated from your parents or guardians. This can be an extremely frightening situation for both the parent and the child. But with a clear mind and a few protocols in place, any situation can be managed.

The key thing to remember if you are ever separated from your parent or guardian is to remain as calm as possible and use the skill of situational awareness until you're reunited at last. Losing your parents is one of the most terrifying things you can deal with, but we will cover the proper techniques you can use to stay safe if it happens.

Setting a Designated Spot

One of the best protocols to have in place, aside from having a phone, is to set a designated meeting spot for the whole group or family. This spot should preferably be large enough to see from a distance, and it should be in the safest location possible. Everyone will be somewhat in a panic if the group is separated, so having the comfort of knowing there is a place to meet will take a bit of the stress off your mind. Let's discuss some of the most ideal places to meet.

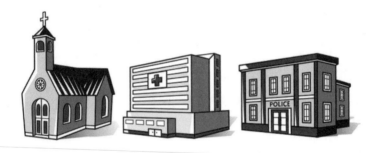

1. **Large churches:** A large church is be a great safe haven for you and the group to meet. During the day, someone is likely to be at the church to accommodate you or your parents if you've become separated. You may even be able to call the church and ask them if anyone has arrived there ahead of you.

2. **Hospital:** Hospitals are usually large and can typically be seen from a distance. If you need directions to the hospital, one of the locals will likely know which way you should go.

3. **Police station:** If there is a police station nearby, you should certainly consider this as an option for a meeting place. If you or your parents show up after getting lost, then the police are legally obligated to help. This can be embarrassing for the parent or guardian, but your safety is far more important.

Finding the Best Place to Go Immediately

If you find yourself separated from your parents or guardian, then you should immediately find a safe place to go in order to collect yourself. Once you calm down, then you can work on getting to the designated spot. If you panic while still standing in the same place you got lost, it could actually prove to be more dangerous and make the situation worse for you and your parents. For example, if you are separated in a crowd of people, then this could be a potential danger because you would look all alone in the eyes of the wrong kind of person. The safest thing to do is immediately get to a public place so that you can calm down, assess the situation, and choose your best option.

1. **Get out of the crowd:** First and foremost, you need to immediately get out of the crowd if that is where you are. Standing in a crowd makes it harder for your parents to find you, and it's far more dangerous because you don't know who's around you.

2. **Stand near a family store/restaurant:** A store where family-oriented people will be is an ideal temporary place for you to stay while assessing the situation. This will be a safer place to be while you figure out where to go or what to do next.

3. **Stay in public view:** In this situation, you need to be cautious of everyone around you, but it's important to stay in a place that is in public and not secluded. Anyone that has bad intentions is more likely to avoid busy areas. If something were to happen to you in public, then someone else would see it happen and be able to help.

The Kind of People to Look For

It's important to maintain caution when it comes to interacting with anyone you don't know. In some cases, finding someone to guide you in the right direction may be the thing that helps you find your parents or helps your parents find you. Along with practicing the previously mentioned tactics, you should find someone to help guide you to a safe location or the designated meeting spot. Here are some people to look for if you need guidance:

1. **Store workers:** Anyone who is working in a uniform is most likely a local and in public view. They will be able to point you in the right direction or maybe even contact help if necessary.

2. **Families:** If anyone is going to help you and show empathy, it will likely be another family. Try your best to find a nearby family and ask them for help. It might also comfort you to be with another kid and their family. Being around other children and their parents during this stressful time can make you feel safer, and you will actually *be* safer near them as well.

3. **Law enforcement and security:** It's extremely important that you're able to identify what a police officer or security guard typically looks like. If you can find a police officer or security guard, then they will be able to keep you safe and out of harm's way. A police officer will also be

able to make contacts and get you where you need to be.

What to Avoid

We have discussed all the places you should go and people you should talk to, but it's equally important that you know what places and people to *avoid* at all costs. These are places where danger usually lurks or there could be people who make the situation worse.

1. **Secluded places:** The danger of being in a hidden, quiet area with no other people around is that you could get kidnapped or hurt and no one else would be around to witness it. There is no advantage to being in secluded areas, so avoid them at all costs.

2. **Abandoned stores or buildings:** Old and abandoned buildings are probably places you would naturally stay away from, but it's still important to point out that these are typically places where dangerous people can hide.

3. **Nightclubs and bars:** Places like nightclubs and bars typically bring in a large variety of people. You need to know that you will probably get no help from them, and they could pose a potential

threat to your safety. Not only that, but the adults at these places are typically drinking alcohol, which can lead to bad thinking. This won't help you find your parents or guardians.

4. **Lone strangers:** This is always a good rule of thumb, but it certainly applies if you're lost. Not every stranger has bad intentions, but if you are separated from your parents in a public area, then it's best that you only make contact with the safe people we talked about earlier, such as families, store workers, and police officers.

5. **Gas stations:** Not only do gas stations often attract thieves, but they also have a history of kidnappings in the past. You have so many other options, so be sure to stay away from all gas stations.

6. **Construction areas:** Construction areas are extremely hazardous to everyone who doesn't have proper gear and training. These areas should be avoided at all costs in order to avoid severe injury or worse.

Cities are large, crowded, and fast-paced, which makes them one of the most common places to get lost. Even when practicing perfect situational awareness, you can still be overwhelmed and find yourself separated and lost very quickly. Using these protocols whenever you are lost will help you approach the situation with a calm mind and execute these learned skills more effectively. If you panic and start running around everywhere without thinking, then you will become even harder to find and might end up in a dangerous place without realizing it.

Staying calm and safe while you try to find your parents or guardians is the most important thing that you can do. If you have a phone, then this will really help ease the anxiety you're likely to experience in this situation, especially if it has Life360. So, plan a designated place to meet nearby before your trip, and you'll be able to use these skills you've learned to make it back to safety.

CHAPTER 3:

HIDING FOR SAFETY

In the previous chapter, we covered choosing a designated safe spot in the event that you become separated from your group. But mistakes happen, and sometimes we forget to designate a spot because we get too busy planning out a fun day. If you don't have a designated safe spot, and you find yourself in a dangerous situation, then there is another survival skill you need to remember. What is that, you may ask? Hiding.

Sometimes, we need to hide in order to keep ourselves safe. In this chapter, we will go over several instances when you may need to hide for safety. Along with hiding for safety, we will cover what to do if you don't feel safe or comfortable around someone, and we'll teach you how to use a superhero calming technique. Here is a secret: Everyone gets scared sometimes — even superheroes and parents. Staying calm is the trick to overcoming your fears.

Best Places to Hide in Public

In scary situations, we simply can't control our fight-or-flight response, and this certainly applies to anyone and everyone. Being lost and separated from a parent is one of the most frightening things you can experience, and feeling scared is a really big emotion! It can cause us to act in ways we normally wouldn't. Sometimes, we cry when we don't mean to or feel too scared to even move. But did you know that sometimes hiding can provide you with comfort and safety? It can! Here are some places you can hide and things you can do if you find yourself in an unfamiliar or dangerous situation:

1. **Nearby restaurant:** If you become separated from your parents or other adults, one of the best things you can do is find a restaurant and sit next to the closest family. Look for families with children. This is a safe option because it allows you to be in a specific place where your parents can find you and may allow you to safely ask for help. Don't feel pressured to tell anyone you're lost if you don't feel comfortable. However, if you build up your courage, ask a waiter to call your parents and let them know where you are. Most likely, they will be happy to help.

2. **Happy and kind-looking families:** If you can't find a restaurant nearby, then look around for a family or at least someone out with their children. If you're too shy to talk, that's okay. Simply walk near them until you find somewhere you feel comfortable.

3. **Hospitals, police stations, or fire departments:** If you ever feel uncomfortable while you're lost and think someone may be following you or someone is just acting weird, then try to locate the nearest hospital, police station, or fire department. The people you meet inside will be willing and ready to help you. You can feel safe while waiting for your parents or guardians.

4. **Churches:** Almost any place you visit will have a local church. If you're ever lost, a church can be a safe place to find shelter and find someone to help you. Apply the same skills, and be sure to tell them your name, your parents' names, and their phone number.

Calming Breathing Techniques

Did you know that learning how to breathe during a scary situation can help you calm down? Practice these breathing techniques and you'll find that you are calmer, more relaxed, and more prepared to make a decision. This is especially helpful if you find yourself in a dangerous situation. Being able to breathe and relax enough to think can help you save your own life just like a real-life superhero.

Take time to practice each one of these breathing techniques and then use them when you feel upset or scared. Getting your body used to them is a key way to automatically calm yourself if you are ever in danger. This will ensure clear, safe, and effective decision-making skills.

1. **Figure-8 breathing:** With this method, breathe calmly and slowly as you visualize the number eight.

   - Visualize the number eight or the infinity symbol, if you're familiar with it. Trace the number or symbol in the air with your finger.
   - Breathe smoothly and slowly, in and out. Make sure you're still tracing the number or symbol in the air as you breathe.
   - To ensure balanced breathing, breathe in during one half of the number or symbol and out during the other half.

2. **Triangle breathing:** Similar to figure-8 breathing, you will visualize a triangle in the air in front of you and trace the triangle with your finger as you breathe slowly in and out.

- Visualize a triangle in front of your face. With your index finger, trace the triangle slowly.

- Now, as you are tracing the triangle, breathe in and out slowly.

- While doing this, keep your breathing slow. Inhale as you trace one side of the triangle, hold your breath at the bottom of the triangle, and exhale as you trace back up to the top of the triangle.

3. **Hand-tracing breathing:** With this method, you will lightly touch and trace your hand as you breathe in and out. This method will help distract you from stress. It uses calming touch and balanced breathing to induce a very calming effect.

Deep breathing using your hand

- Place your hand on your lap with the palm facing up.
- Start tracing the outline of your hand, going in between each finger and breathing in and out during the process.
- Lightly touch your palm, starting from the outside and spiraling to the inside in a circle.
- Repeat this process while keeping a slow and balanced breathing cycle.

4. **Belly breathing:** With this method, you will practice slow and controlled breathing using your belly.

- Start by inhaling through your nose for 3 to 4 seconds.
- Imagine your belly is like a balloon and you are filling it up by inhaling.
- Pause your breathing for 2 seconds, and exhale slowly through your mouth.
- Imagine that you are letting the air out of the balloon, and you should feel your belly go down.
- Repeat this process, and you'll get even better at controlled breathing as you practice this method.

Calling for Help

Sometimes, we can get so scared that we forget everything we are supposed to do. That's okay. Even if we don't remember all the steps or skills we learn, we can still do a very basic thing to help ourselves in a dangerous situation—calling for help. Everyone needs help sometimes. Calling out for help can get you what you need quickly. This is especially useful if you feel panicked. Finding help quickly will allow you calm down and realize you are no longer in danger.

1. **Go to a public location and use a phone:** If you can, safely locate a public business, and ask a worker there if you can use their phone to call 911. This will let the worker know that you need help. This can help you feel better knowing you did a great job and found yourself the help you needed.

2. **Find a police officer:** Your safety is important. Knowing how to take care of yourself is awesome. If you are in a city, you may be able to find a local police officer to help you. They are trained to help you and will do what they can to make you feel safe.

3. **Don't run around screaming for help:** Try not to scream or yell for help. This might seem like a great way to get an adult's attention, but it could get the attention of someone who wants to harm you. Remember the skills we mentioned before, and try to find a mom or family to ask for help immediately.

If you utilize these methods, along with practiced breathing techniques, to stay calm, you increase your chances of safely managing the situation more effectively. If you and your family know you will be traveling, ask them if you can have a device to carry with you in case of emergencies. Your parents or guardians can add apps like Life360 to find you if you become separated from them. Remember to memorize your address and parents' phone numbers. This is very important information if you are ever lost and need to ask an adult for help.

CHAPTER 4:

BASIC SELF-DEFENSE

We can't talk about survival skills without talking about self-defense. There are so many things that can happen that may require self-defense. Self-defense doesn't always happen in physical combat—it can mean anything from evading a dangerous person to scaring away an animal. You can also defend yourself by buying more time until you can get help. In this chapter, we will talk about skills you can use to scare someone away, avoid someone, or get attention if you're in danger. As a child, it is always best that you avoid physical fights if at all possible.

Basic Evasion Techniques

If you are ever in a situation where a dangerous person or animal is trying to harm you, then your best option is to get away. You may feel like being brave and fighting off whatever is trying to hurt you, but it's always a great choice to evade first and fight last. Here are ways that you can defend yourself just by evading:

1. **Wave and smile:** If a person is going to try to hurt you, they probably think you're alone. A great way to make them think you're with someone is by smiling and waving to a nearby person. Pick someone random in the crowd or no one at all. Now, give a smile, wave, and start walking in that direction. Something like this will make a dangerous person too scared to mess with you because they'll think you aren't alone.

2. **Run away:** You may find yourself scared because a stranger seems to be following you. If this is true, you should run to a safe place like a busy restaurant or store. Tell a worker you're in danger, and they should help you.

3. **Pay attention:** When you're running, it's easy to get lost because you're scared. Try your best to pay attention to where you're going. If you get lost, you might end up running into a dangerous area that you shouldn't be in.

Words to Use to Get Attention

Sometimes, you can do everything possible to stay safe but still find yourself in a dangerous situation. You may do everything right and still get attention from a bad person. If this happens, just remember that other families will most likely help you. Learn these skills to let other people know you are in danger:

Things to say to others:

- **"Someone help me. I'm scared."**
- **"I'm being chased by someone who wants to hurt me."**
- **"This person is trying to hurt me."**

Things to say to the person chasing you:

- **"Leave me alone!"**
- **"I don't know you!"**

Where to Go and What to Do After Running Away

You ran away, found safety, and now you need to hide until you can get help. Make sure you don't go back to where everything started. The person who is trying to hurt you or scared you may be there again, and you don't want that. Here are some places where you can go so that you can get help while you hide:

1. **Hide in the public eye:** Make sure that you are around people. You don't need to be alone if someone is following you.

2. **Go to a store:** Once you think you have gotten away, you should find a store and get a store worker to help you. Tell them you are in danger, and they will call for help. Don't leave.
3. **Find a family with kids:** After you get away, or even if you're being followed, find a family and ask them for help. They will help you or keep you safe while you are hiding.
4. **Tell them what the stranger looks like:** If a stranger is following or chasing you, try to remember what they look like and what they're wearing. Once you find a worker or family to help you, you can tell them so that they know who to look for. They will also know who to keep away from you.

Always try your best to escape a dangerous stranger, and never give up. No matter how big or scary the stranger is, you can get away if you remember these skills. The main things you should know in order to evade are:

- **Get everyone's attention.**
- **Yell, escape, and hide.**
- **Stay around a lot of people.**
- **Get help.**

SECTION 2:

THE WILDERNESS

This section will cover survival skills you can use while camping or hiking in the woods. Here are some things that you should have while camping or hiking:

- Cell phone
- GPS
- Compass
- Water
- Matches
- Lighters

- Bright cloth
- Map
- Whistle
- Air horn
- Flashlight

Here are things you should know:

- Where the roads are
- The direction of springs, rivers, or streams
- Where you set up camp and how it's marked on the map

CHAPTER 5:

WHAT TO DO WHEN LOST IN THE WOODS

Now that we've covered survival skills for the city, we'll learn more about what it takes to survive in the woods. The first thing you need to know about survival in the woods is what to do if you get lost. Being lost in the woods is very different from being lost in the city because other people are less likely to be around. Finding your way to safety can be tricky, even if you have someone with you. In this chapter, you will learn how to navigate the woods without putting yourself in an even worse situation.

Basic Directional Skills

One of the biggest dangers in the wilderness is that your sense of direction can be easily confused. In a forest or thickly wooded area, the trees will all look the same, making it very tricky to stay on the right path. Sometimes, you can use things like the sun or moon to help identify which direction you should walk to find a road, but the sun or moon won't help much if you can't see them through the tall trees or don't know where the roads are.

When you go camping or are in the woods, it's a good idea to study the area to know which direction the streets are. This will help you if you get lost because you will know which path you should travel using your other survival skills learned in this book. In this section, you will learn how to find your way to safety if you're lost in the wilderness.

1. **Use the sun or moon as a guide:** One important thing to know here is that the sun and moon rise in the east and set in the west. Using that information, you should be able to locate the sun or moon and determine the right direction of travel.

2. **Use a compass:** Every time you go camping or spend time in the wilderness, you should always be equipped with tools that can help you find your way if you get lost. A compass is an excellent tool for figuring out where north, south, east, and west are. If you plan ahead and know where the road or your campsite is, you should be able to point the compass and travel in the correct direction.

3. **Choose one direction, and stick to it:** Make sure to stick with your travel direction. If you are not confident with your chosen path, you should take a few minutes to figure out your best option and then stay with it. If you start walking a different way every time you come to a stop, you will almost certainly put yourself in a worse situation.

Listen for Sounds

If you're lost in the woods and can't remember where your camp and the roads are, you should rely on your ears to help you out. When you're in the woods, sounds that really stand out are ones that don't belong in the wilderness. Here are some things you should stop and listen for as you walk. Doing this could give you a clue to where nearby people are or, even better, your camp.

1. **Vehicles:** You can usually hear moving cars passing by if you are not too deep in the woods. If you hear a car, then move in that direction. Head toward the sound of the vehicles, which will lead you to a road. If you know which road it is, you can hopefully get someone's help or even make it back to camp or your car.

2. **Constant walking:** Humans are usually the only ones that move at a continuous pace. Stop and listen while traveling in your chosen direction to see if someone else is walking in the distance. Remember, if you are lost, your parents or friends will be doing everything they can to find you, and you may be able to hear them.

3. **Voices:** If you are lost, you can be sure that your parents, guardians, or friends are looking for

you. They will be yelling for you, which is something else you should listen for. You should immediately walk in that direction if you hear the sound of voices.

4. **Flowing water:** Depending on where you are in the world, there could be streams or areas with flowing water. Streams, springs, and rivers are significant landmarks that may help your family or friends find you more easily. Sometimes, if you listen very carefully, you can hear the water flowing.

Leaving a Trail

One of the most important things you can do while lost in the woods is try not to get even more lost than you already are. It can be scary to get lost, and you may start to panic. The best thing to remember is that you can and will find your way out as long as you stay calm and don't make things worse. If you think you know where you should go, you must remember the way you came from so that you don't go in the wrong direction or somewhere you've already been. Here are ways that you can leave a trail for yourself or anyone who may be looking for you:

1. **Create small piles of leaves or sticks:** As you walk through the woods, stop every 5 minutes to create a mark and listen. Doing this will show you that you've been in that area. You can clear a bare spot on the ground and make a pile of leaves or small sticks. Make the spot stand out from the environment.

2. **Hang bright pieces of cloth or socks on branches:** If you're prepared, you should have some colorful socks or shirts that you can hang on trees as you walk. This will help you remember where you've been, and they can easily be seen by anyone looking for you.

3. **Mark your direction of travel:** Any time you make a turn or change your direction of travel, make an arrow on the ground using sticks or

leaves. This will help anyone looking for you continue in the same direction.

Make Loud Noises

As you walk through the woods, you need to do anything to help your parents or caregivers know what direction you are heading. One thing that your parents will be doing is using their ears to find you. The more you make a lot of noise, the faster they will find you. Here are some ways to make noise so that your parents know it's you:

1. **Yell:** Adults may sometimes tell you to use your inside voice, but if you're lost in the woods, this is when you use the loudest voice you can. It doesn't matter what you yell — you can simply scream out names or noises until someone finds you.

2. **Use your whistle:** If you came prepared, you should have a whistle. While you're walking, you should blow the whistle a lot. A loud whistle blow in the woods will stand out and should be loud enough for your parents to hear even from far away. Use your whistle the whole time, and your parents or guardians will be able to listen for it and find you.

3. **Use an air horn:** If you didn't bring a whistle, maybe you have an air horn. These are also very loud and can be heard from far away. Use your air horn just like the whistle, and your parents will be able to hear where you are.

4. **Walk loudly:** Maybe you forgot your whistle or air horn. That's alright! You can use sticks, rocks, and trees to make noise for others to hear. You can kick sticks, throw rocks, or hit trees with sticks. While walking through the woods, make sure you are careful not to trip and fall while making a lot of noise with your feet.

The most important thing for you to remember is that you shouldn't give up. You can find your way out, and you will find your parents, friends, or guardians. When you're lost and feeling afraid, make sure to stop and breathe. After you've calmed down, start thinking about the last place you remember seeing before you got lost. Now, you can look at what you see in front of you, and you might find something you saw before you felt lost.

If you think you know the direction you should go, slowly move in that direction and don't change your mind. If it is too dark to see, it's best to stay in one place so you don't get hurt or lost. Use everything you have learned in this chapter, and you will be able to find your way out of the woods or help others find you.

CHAPTER 6:

ANIMAL EVASION

If you are camping, hiking, or even lost in the woods, there is always the chance you may encounter wild animals. This may seem like a scary situation, but there are survival skills that you can use to evade these dangerous animals. The first thing to do is to try to stay as calm as you can. There is a good chance that the animal will leave if you stay calm and don't make any sudden movements. If this doesn't happen, there are other skills you can use to defend yourself. In this chapter, we will show you some essential survival skills that will help you evade and defend yourself when encountering a wild animal.

Using noise and scare tactics

It can be a terrifying situation to encounter wild animals in the wild. The truth is that most animals are actually terrified of humans. One key thing to remember is that you should always try to keep animals away from you. You can actually do things as you walk through the woods that will reduce your chances of even seeing a wild animal. Here are some survival skills that you can use to keep animals from ever seeing you and will likely make them avoid you:

1. **Loud walking:** This one is straightforward because you will probably already be doing this. You can even make it fun by kicking up leaves, kicking a rock when you see it, and hitting trees with sticks. Simply doing these things will lower the chances of you ever walking up on an animal because they will be able to hear you from far away and go in another direction.

2. **Loud talking and singing:** You might have a fantastic voice, so why not let the animals hear it while you walk through the woods? Animals may think your voice is beautiful, but it will also scare them away because they fear you. You can walk calmly if you're talking or singing because you probably won't see any wild animals.

3. **Noisemakers:** Here is a time when you can use the whistle that you packed because you're savvy and prepared! Nearly all animals dislike loud noises. Whistles are perfect to use while walking because if an animal hears a whistle, they know something is in the woods that doesn't live there, which scares them. Suppose you blow on your whistle every time you stop for a moment. If you do this, you will definitely not encounter many wild animals.

4. **Scents:** Many wild animals navigate by using their noses. Animals know what everything in the woods should smell like. When camping or hiking, make sure to put a scent on yourself,

such as lotion or sunscreen. If the wind blows and animals smell you, they will run away before getting close.

Recognizing Animal Tracks, Manure, and Markings

Before you ever go hiking or camping with your family or friends, make sure you know what kind of animals live in the area you're going to be visiting. This will help you prepare for any specific encounters with a wild animal. It will also help you decide which travel route to take because you don't want to follow an animal and surprise it. Here are some survival tactics you can learn to identify animal tracks and avoid animal encounters:

1. **Tracks:** Animal tracks are footprints you can find on moist areas of the ground. If you look at the animal track and see where the toes are, you will know which direction they are walking.

2. **Manure:** Animal scat is simply manure. An excellent thing to pay attention to about animal manure is how dry it is. If the scat seems very dry, it's safe to say that the animal that left it there is probably far away by now, and that scat is old. On the other hand, if the manure is still fresh and seems wet or moist, then that's a sign

that an animal was just there, and you should leave the area as soon as possible.

3. **Bedding:** This is something you won't usually come across, but it can be helpful if you notice where an animal has been sleeping. You might see an area of grass that has been pressed down, which should look brighter or different from the grass around it.

4. **Markings:** This is something hunters usually use to find animals, but it can also be helpful for you to avoid them. If you look at the trees while you're walking, you may see one with some of the bark rubbed off. These spots stand out because you should now be able to see the light-brown wood of the inside of the tree. This will let you know that a large animal has been close to that area.

Knowing How to React to Certain Animals

As said before, it is always a good idea to learn which animals will be in the area before you travel. The more you know about the animals that live there, the more prepared you will be if you encounter one. There are more wild animals in the wilderness than you could ever imagine. Still, there are some animals you are more likely to see than others, which can be extremely dangerous if you come upon a predator. Here are some animals to look for and where you can usually find them:

1. **Snakes:** Snakes are part of the reptile family and can be one of the most dangerous animals to encounter in the wild. These reptiles hide under rocks, swim in the water, and even climb trees. They are very quiet and often prefer tall, thick grass. What makes reptiles so tricky is how many there are and how easy it is to walk up on one without seeing it. Don't make any fast or sudden movements; if you ever encounter a snake, slowly back away. If you are too scared to move, you can stay as still as possible, and it should eventually slither away.

2. **Bears:** This could be the most terrifying animal encounter you will ever have. Even though

seeing a bear is highly unlikely, it could still happen, and it's good to know what you should do in this case. Most bears are afraid of humans. Unless you seem like a threat to the bear, it will usually run away. Bears are extremely dangerous; if you see a bear, the only option is to leave. They are excellent climbers, swimmers, and runners. It is essential to make a lot of noise as you walk so that bears can know to stay away from you. If you see one, calmly back away and don't make any sudden moves. Leave the area as quietly as possible without doing anything that could scare the bear.

3. **Coyotes:** Coyotes are very common. If you ever see one, the best thing you can do is slowly walk away as you would with any other animal. Coyotes are fast runners, but they are usually more afraid of you and run away like the others. If the coyote starts chasing you and you don't have anything to defend yourself with, you should find a tree you can climb.

Finding Items to Defend Yourself With

The first thing you should always do during a wild animal encounter is stay calm and attempt to walk away. Usually this will work, or the animal will run away first. Sometimes, an animal may think that you're trying to hurt it, and it may attack you. If you ever find yourself in this situation, the best thing you can do is keep your eyes on the animal and don't fall to the ground. Here are a few items that could help if you ever have to defend yourself against an animal attacking you.

1. **Sticks:** A stick can be one of your best weapons if an animal gets too close to you. Before that happens, swing the stick back and forth at the animal, which could even be enough to scare it off. Make sure you don't throw the stick at the animal, as this could make it mad if you hit it, and then you wouldn't have your stick to defend yourself.

2. **Rocks:** It's always a good idea to keep a few rocks in your pocket if you find them, just in case you find an animal following or chasing you. You can use rocks to scare the animal away. Be mindful of throwing rocks at a wild animal. If you hit the animal, you could make it

angrier, and it might try to hurt you. But in some instances, if you hit the wild animal, this could cause it to run away. Always use caution when throwing any object at a wild animal to defend yourself.

3. **Backpack or hiking bag:** Hopefully, you prepared for your camping or hiking trip and brought a bag. You can use the bag to keep your body away from the animal and lower the chance of it hurting you. You could also use it to defend yourself if an animal is chasing you. If you feel like your bag could hurt it, and you don't have a stick, you can even swing the bag at the animal to try and scare it away.

In this chapter, you learned survival tactics you can use if you ever encounter a wild animal. Before you defend yourself, always try to stay calm and walk away. Most of the time, an animal won't attack and will run away. In rare cases, you may find yourself dealing with an animal that feels threatened or angry. If that happens, make sure you do what you can to keep your distance by using the weapons you found in the woods. Many animals spend time around areas with water, such as streams, springs, and rivers. Be mindful of your surroundings if you're in one of these areas.

The following chapters will teach you several helpful survival skills to know when in the wilderness, regardless of the situation. The survival skills in these chapters are things you can use when camping, hiking, and enjoying water activities.

CHAPTER 7:

HOW TO BUILD A FIRE

When you think of camping or being in the woods, you naturally think of campfires. So, it's only natural that we begin with one of the most essential skills when it comes to survival in the wilderness. Not only do campfires allow us to cook food, but they can also serve as valuable warmth or be used as signals. In the colder months, temperatures can drop so low that you can get sick if you don't have a way to stay warm during the night. This is why even a small campfire can be crucial to your survival.

If you are lost in the woods, a campfire could be bright enough for someone to notice it in the distance and come find you. No matter what it's for, knowing how to build a fire with minimal resources is a whole new challenge. Building a fire can be almost impossible if you don't truly understand what it takes to make one. In this chapter, we will cover the things that a fire needs in order to exist. Further along, you will learn how to find the materials to start a fire, keep it burning, lower the amount of smoke, and stay safe around a fire.

Elements of Fire

When you think of fire, you might just think that they are hot and need to have some fuel to keep burning. If you don't know what makes up a fire, it'll be hard to understand why you're struggling to start one or keep it burning once you've created one. Knowing these characteristics makes it easier to understand how and where to build a fire, and this information will also be helpful if you ever need to put a fire out for safety reasons. Understanding the following characteristics will help you safely manage fires throughout your life, no matter the situation. Here are the three different elements of fire:

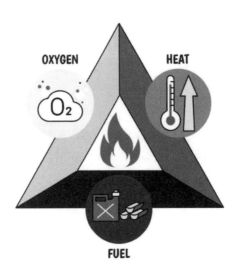

1. **Heat:** Fire needs energy in the form of a heat source. Once the fire is going, heat will dry out nearby materials and warm the air.

2. **Oxygen:** A fire needs oxygen because it combines with carbon inside the materials you feed the fire, creating a chemical reaction.

3. **Fuel:** Fire needs the chemical reaction between oxygen and carbon to happen for it to ignite. This carbon is found in fuel sources such as wood, paper, fabrics, and other combustible items. Without fuel, a fire will eventually go out because there is no more carbon to combine with oxygen.

Finding Your Fire Materials

Now that you know what a fire needs, it's time to find those items and put them to use. First, we will discuss the best things to use to make starting a fire easier for you. Everything you need to create fire can typically be found in the woods as long as you're patient and pay close attention to your surroundings. When you're looking for these items, it's best to search in dry areas, and you want items that are already dead and on the ground. Remember: A fire needs heat, carbon materials, and airflow (oxygen). Here are things that you should look for and where you can find them:

1. **Tinder:** Tinder is the small piece of carbon that you need to create the fire. Things like pine needles, leaves, and tree bark can all serve as tinder. You can also use dry grass, found nearly anywhere, such as on your lawn after it has been cut. Remember that tinder is temporary and only used to get the bigger materials burning. Here are several different items that you can use as tinder to start your fire:

   - **Lint**
   - **Toilet paper**
   - **Dry pine needles**

- **Pinecones**
- **Cardboard**
- **Small, dry twigs**
- **Dry bark**
- **Cotton**
- **Animal manure**

2. **Kindling:** Kindling is what you will use on top of the tinder to keep the fire going until you can get it hot enough to start adding larger items such as logs and branches. Make sure any kindling you find is small and dry or else it won't burn hot enough to keep the fire going. Here are some items that you can use as kindling:

- **Large pinecones**
- **Cardboard**
- **A newspaper tied into a knot**
- **Small twigs**
- **Twig shavings**
- **Potato chips**

3. **Logs:** You will need small wooden logs and branches to keep your fire going for a long time. Make sure these logs are as dry as possible and small in size. If you try to use moist logs or logs

that are too large, it will kill the heat of the fire and smother it.

4. **Bow:** A bow was one of the most common ways to start a fire in ancient times. You can make a bow using two straight, dry sticks paired with something like a shoelace. We will cover the bow method in further detail in the next section.

Fire-Starting Methods

You've gathered all the material that a fire needs. Now what? You still need to know how to combine these items with methods that will create a chemical reaction to start the fire. You will learn how to use friction techniques to generate enough heat to ignite a fire. Many fire-starting kits are very easy to use, and if you can get one of these, you should definitely make them a part of your emergency bag or camping kit. The following methods will use a variety of items, some of which you can find in your surroundings in the woods.

1. **Flint and steel:** Flint and steel is one of the easiest ways to start a fire, and it's used mainly by hikers and campers. This method involves using a piece of steel and a flint to create sparks when you strike them together. There are many

flint and steel fire-starting kits that you can buy from your local hardware or sporting goods store. Here is how you use a flint and steel to create fire:

- First, go ahead and gather some tinder and kindling, as mentioned before, and form a small cone-shaped pile.

- Next, take a group of sticks and stack them against and beside each other to form a cone shape. This will be your actual campfire.

- Now, we have the base and structure of the fire set up. Place a pile of dry tinder on the ground next to the structure. Make sure you put your tinder directly next to the cone so that it's easier to move the tinder when the time comes.

- Place your flint on top of the tinder, or hold it just above it.

- Strike the flint in a downward motion, which will create sparks if done correctly. The sparks will eventually ignite the tinder, which will give you the start to your fire.

- Slowly add more tinder to the fire, and move the pile underneath your cone of sticks. Now you have the start to your fire.

- Over time, as your fire starts to grow, all your sticks will have ignited. As necessary, you can slowly begin stacking larger sticks over the others in a cone shape.

2. **Water bottle:** With this method, you can use a water bottle as a magnifying glass to start your fire. All you need is some tinder or a piece of paper if you have it.

- Take your piece of paper or tinder and lay it on the ground.
- Take the bottle of water and hold it over the tinder. While doing this, ensure you are lining up the sun with the curve of the bottle.
- You should start seeing the sun heating up your tinder and causing it to smoke within seconds. As this happens, gently blow on the smoky tinder while you slowly add more tinder to the pile.
- As you blow on the smoke, keep the sunlight and bottle lined up on the tinder like a magnifying glass. If done properly over time, the smoke turns into fire.

- Now, you can carefully push your pile of tinder underneath your nearby fire pit and add kindling to it.

3. **Flashlight: This could be one of the best methods because you should definitely have a flashlight packed in your bag. This method is one of the fastest and easiest methods to use if it is done correctly.**

  - First, take the flashlight glass off and pull the shiny cone part out.
  - Next, stuff any tinder into the hole of the shiny cone, and make sure you have more tinder near you.
  - Now that your shiny cone is stuffed with tinder, start to point the large end of the cone toward the sun until you begin to see the tinder smoke. If you continue to shine it toward the sun, a fire should start, and you can then continue adding tinder on top.
  - Soon, you will be able to slowly add kindling, and you can start building a larger fire as needed.

How to Create Less Smoke in Your Fire

If you're lost, you may want your fire to create as much smoke as possible so that someone can find you in the woods. But if you're just camping or exploring, you should seek to create as little smoke as possible for safety reasons. Excessive smoke can scare others or be hazardous to your health. Here are some ways to build a fire with less smoke:

1. **Use dry wood:** Make sure you're only using dry wood that has been on the ground for a while. Any wood that is green or still attached to a living tree may contain too much moisture, causing a very smoky fire.

2. **Don't burn debris:** Debris is anything that isn't natural. If you try to burn clothes, bottles, paper, or plastic, it will create a lot of smoke because of the chemicals inside these products. This kind of smoke isn't good to breathe in, so try to only use natural items like wood and dry grass.

3. **Good airflow:** If your fire doesn't have good airflow, it may start smoking more because it's dying. To help keep your fire alive and prevent smoking, add small amounts of wood to it as you need. If you pile too much wood or grass onto your fire, you may accidentally smother it.

4. **Don't use pine:** Any kind of pine tree will have oils inside that cause a very smoky fire. This

smoke can be toxic to your body, so it's best not to burn pine wood or needles. If you are in a survival situation and it's the only wood available, make sure you limit your time around the smoky fire.

How to Safely Put Out a Fire

Fires can be hazardous if not managed properly. Even though it may have been hard to start a fire, you still can't leave a fire going for too long unattended. A key thing to remember is that it's much easier to manage a fire than to extinguish a fire that's already out of control. Here are ways to safely put out a fire if you don't need it or you have to leave the area for an extended period:

1. **Prepare a safe fire area:** The first step to safely putting out a fire is to safely manage the fire from the start. When you are preparing the place for your fire, get rid of any pine needles or leaves around your fire area. You need to create a circle of dry ground or dirt around the fire pit so that the fire can't escape that area.

2. **Wet the ground:** Another good safety measure is to wet the ground around the fire. This

reduces the chances of the fire spreading past that area.

3. **Use water:** You're very smart and probably know that water can put out a fire. If you're done with your fire and don't need it anymore, you can pour water on it. Make sure that there are no more embers or smoke left before leaving the fire area.

4. **Smother with dirt:** Another great method to put out a small fire is to take all of its oxygen away. A simple way to do this is gathering some dirt and throwing it on the fire. Once you've thrown enough dirt onto the fire, it will start to smoke more and go out. If it's an emergency, you can also use a wet towel to quickly smother and put out the fire.

Remember: While fire is a great thing to have, it can also be very dangerous. Building a fire can be hard to do, and when you finally get it started, you may not want to put it out. But leaving a fire while you're gone for a long time is a real danger that can get out of hand. If you haven't cleared an area of dry grass, leaves, and anything else that could catch fire, you are risking your fire getting out of hand. Any time you start a fire, you should have water ready at all times and keep the area around the fire clear of any materials that could burn.

CHAPTER 8:

HOW TO BUILD A SHELTER

Creating a shelter in the woods offers you more than just a roof over your head when you're camping or lost. Having shelter around you can also keep you hidden from wild animals or other dangers. Weather can make a camping trip go bad, and a tent may not hold up well enough against the wind or rain. In times like these, knowing how to build a shelter is a very useful skill to have. Not only does shelter offer you protection, but it also can provide comfort if you're ever lost in the woods. Being inside a shelter protects you from harsh weather or animals and helps keep you warm from the cold. There are many ways to build a shelter while camping or when you're lost simply by using the environment around you.

Choose a Shelter Location

A shelter is very important because it will protect you from wind, cold, and rain. Exposure to these things can make you sick, and nobody wants that—especially in an emergency. Before you can build an effective shelter, you need to consider how comfortable you feel with heights. In some cases, you may want to seek shelter on a wide branch of a tree. This can help protect you from ground-based animals such as bears, wolves, and other roaming predators. However, if heights are not your thing, you can feel comfortable in a grounded shelter as well. Here are some things to know before you start setting up camp:

- First, find the perfect spot. When considering where you want to set up your shelter, you need to look for a small clearing, preferably near water but not too close to it. Sometimes, creeks and rivers can rise during the night, and the last thing you want is for your shelter to become flooded with water.

- Another thing to look for when finding the perfect spot for a shelter is a space that already offers some form of natural shelter. This could look like trees that have low-lying branches to create the beginning of a roof or a small hill with trees close by. The hill acts as a natural wall and requires you to find fewer materials.

- Lastly, avoid setting up your shelter near an obvious animal nest or den. Even if you think the nest may be abandoned, it is best not to take that chance. Animals can become aggressive if they think you mean them harm or you're on their territory. Nests can be found is trees, branches, or holes in the ground, and many can be identified by unusual amounts of markings or scat.

Types of Shelters

Now that you've picked where you want to build your shelter, you need to think of what kind of shelter you want to build. Choosing the type of shelter will depend on what you need for your specific situation. If you just need shelter from the weather for a short time, you can often take cover under large trees. In some places, you may even find small caves that you can use. Here are a few different ways you can build your own shelter using materials in the wilderness and some ways to use the environment as a natural shelter:

1. **Natural shelters:** Natural shelters can be found in unexpected places. Like you, animals outgrow their homes and find new places to go. This allows them to leave behind pre-made shelters that can help us in our time of need.

- **Caves:** Caves are one of nature's wonders and can offer the perfect shelter. Caves are already formed with walls and a roof that will protect you from rain, wind, and severe cold. It's important to inspect the cave before entering. Make noise before you go in to scare animals that may be inside to make them come out. Enter slowly, making noise the whole way. If the cave goes deeper than a few feet, do not attempt to go any further in. Stay close enough to see the entrance of the cave. If you build a fire inside the cave, you will need to have proper ventilation.

- **Cavities in trees:** Sometimes, animals will create large open spaces inside of a tree trunk or a tree is naturally shaped that way. This is very helpful, as it can provide you with shelter. Inspect a tree for any animals such as birds, chipmunks, squirrels, or mice. If there are no nests, then you can take shelter inside the tree and rest for the night. To make the space more comfortable, you can add leaves and grass.

- **Large fallen trees:** When you are wandering in the woods, you might come across a fallen tree. These can be perfect makeshift shelters. When a large enough tree falls, there are sometimes large gaps between the ground and the tree trunk. You can create an even bigger space by digging out more loose dirt and leaves. The idea is to create a space big enough for you to fit comfortably under the tree but not so big that it could cause the tree to slide down further.

- **Pine trees:** These are trees that you may not want to burn, but the pine needles on the ground offer a naturally soft place to sit. The amount of coverage that a pine tree can offer is great as well. If you have a tarp, you can lay it across some of the low branches for extra cover. Some pine trees keep needles on their branches even through the wintertime. This will help provide cover from the weather.

2. **Tarp tent:** If you came into the wilderness prepared, then that means you should have some kind of tarp or emergency blanket in your bag. With this tarp or blanket, you can easily

make a tent that will provide cover using nearby trees for support.

- First, find two trees that are close to each other. They don't have to be huge trees. They just need to be large and strong enough to hold up your tarp or blanket.
- Second, take your emergency cord or rope that you brought in your bag and tie each end around one of the trees. Make sure that you tie the rope or cord low enough that your tarp will reach the ground when you throw it over.
- Third, throw your tarp over the cord or rope, and adjust the rope if it's too high or low. The tarp needs to reach the ground.

- Last, find four rocks or logs that are big enough to put on each corner of the tarp. This will make the tarp stay open in a tent shape and keep it from closing on you.

3. **A-frame shelter:** An A-frame shelter may be one of the easiest shelters to build. All you need is a tarp or emergency blanket. This kind of shelter will help block any cold wind and help you stay dry during rain or snow.

   - First, find a low-hanging branch that is strong and unbroken. You can also find a fallen tree to create this kind of shelter.
   - Second, throw your tarp or emergency blanket over the branch or fallen tree.
   - Last, anchor each corner of the tarp on the ground with a heavy rock or nearby log.

4. **Lean-to shelter:** This is a very easy shelter to build and is very useful if you didn't bring a poncho, tarp, or emergency blanket. To build this shelter, you won't need any tools or materials. Everything that you need can be gathered from your environment. This shelter will help you stay dry and block the cold wind. It can also be good for hiding from animals and protecting yourself if you need.

- First, find a standing or fallen tree. This will be the structure of your shelter, and it needs to be strong enough to support a lot of logs and branches.
- Second, find several branches and logs that are long enough to sit under. They should be longer than you.
- Last, lean the logs and branches that you found against the standing or fallen tree. Keep leaning them against the tree until all the gaps around the tree have been filled. Leave a small gap that's still large enough for you to enter and exit.

Finding Shelter Materials

Now that you've chosen where you want our camp to be, you need to start gathering the materials to build your shelter. It's important to choose the right items when building your shelter, and it's equally important to assemble your shelter correctly. If you don't pick the right materials, you could expose yourself to the weather or risk getting hurt.

1. **Leaves**: Gather large, broad leaves. The bigger the leaf, the better. Larger leaves ensure that you cover more area for less.

2. **Sticks:** When you want to create a shelter, you need to remember that you aren't just trying to build a giant fort. You want to build something that protects you from the elements. When you're searching for materials for your shelter, find sticks that are not too big and not too small. Think about Eeyore from *Winnie-the-Pooh* and how he set up his sticks.

3. **Clothing:** Consider using any extra clothing such as jackets, raincoats, or hoodies. If it isn't essential for you to wear, then you can use it as a covering for your shelter.

4. **Vines:** Finding thick vines can be especially helpful since they're a form of natural string.

You can tie them together to make them longer or shorten them as needed. You can use them to tie sticks together, or if you find enough, you can loop them through your shelter to create walls and a roof.

Now that you know how to find a shelter or build one, you're prepared to stay safe and comfortable in the woods no matter what your situation is. Make sure that you provide a warm base for yourself no matter what kind of shelter you find or build. You can do this by taking all the leaves or pine needles that you gathered and placing them on the ground inside your shelter.

CHAPTER 9:

HOW TO FIND WATER

Our bodies are made up of mostly water, so finding water is one of the most important survival skills that you will need. We're all supposed to drink a little over 8 cups of water every day. Water is important for your health, and if you don't have it, you will eventually get very sick. When searching for water, there are many signs that you can look for that will lead you there. There are also some neat tricks that you can use to collect water from the ground, from wet morning grass, and even from the rain. Here are all the ways that you can find sources of water:

Signals of Nearby Water Sources

When out in the woods, you already know that you need to be aware of your surroundings. Well, this is where your situational awareness will be extremely helpful. First, you need to under-stand that every living thing needs some type of water to survive. We are all made up of water, and you can find water in all areas of the Earth if you know where to look or what to do to find it. Here are some of the signals that you should look for when you are trying to find a water source in the wild:

1. **Wildlife:** Animals are just like us when it comes to needing water. They're always on their feet and exploring, so they know the area better than you do, and they can help you find water. If you find animal tracks, you can be sure that those animal tracks will eventually lead you to water. If you see birds or other animals going in one direction, then this could be a potential sign of a water source.

2. **Fresh, green grass:** Something else you can look for to find water is green grass. Water is very important for plants, and they also need a lot of sunlight. Thick green grass is getting lots of

water and sunlight, which means there could be a natural spring or watering hole nearby.

3. **Insects:** If you're starting to see a lot of insects nearby, such as mosquitoes, gnats, and beetles, you are probably getting closer to a water source.

4. **Sounds:** There aren't many sounds in the woods, which makes it easy to hear things that you normally couldn't. As you're looking, you should pause periodically. If you listen very carefully, you may be able to hear a running river nearby.

Creating Your Own Water

Maybe you've searched for a long time, and you are certain there are no water sources nearby. Don't worry because there are ways that you can get water from under the ground, on the grass, and even from the sky. Of course, water like this would need to be cleaned before you could actually drink it, but we will cover that soon. Here are some ways that you can obtain water without an actual large water source:

1. **Underground water:** You've probably never thought about this before, but there's actually

water under a lot of the ground that we walk on. In order to find this underground water, look for things like moist or muddy ground. Once you find ground that seems moist or muddy, start digging a hole. Eventually, if you dig deep enough, you will start to see some water seep into the hole. After cleaning this muddy water, it will be good to drink.

2. **Collect rainwater:** Collecting rainwater will depend on your luck and the weather. If it does rain while you are lost or camping, then you can collect rainwater in many ways. Many leaves will collect the water inside, and you can even dig a small hole to collect water if you need. If you have a tarp with you, then you can also use that to collect water by tying it up to catch the rain.

3. **Morning dew:** In the morning, you may notice that grass is usually slightly wet. You can actually take a cloth or towel and collect the dew from any plants or grass. This dew is essentially water created by condensation. This sounds gross, but if you absolutely need water, then you should do this. Once you collect as much dew on your cloth as you can, you can squeeze it into a container or onto your tarp. Remember

that you still need to clean and purify all water that you find before drinking it.

Water Purification

When you are alone, it's very important to remember that not all water is safe for you to drink. Sometimes, you will find water that needs to be purified before you can safely drink it. There are some simple ways for you to purify your water using materials you may already have with you or that you can find around you.

Below is a step-by-step guide on how to purify your water if you have a water bottle or any other plastic bottle.

DIY Water Filter

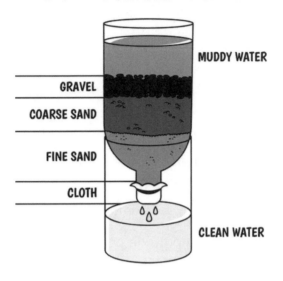

First step: Cut your water bottle in half.

Second step: Find small pebbles, leaves, and sand, if possible.

Third step: This will sound gross, but if you have a clean sock in your bag, get it out because it helps make a great filter. If you don't have a sock, then you can rip off a small piece of your shirt or jacket.

Fourth step: Take your piece of fabric and stretch it across the opening of the bottom portion of the bottle. Flip the neck of the bottle into the bottom half.

Fifth step: Layer your contents in this exact order: first sand, then leaves, and lastly, add in your pebbles.

Sixth step: Slowly pour in water.

It may seem unlikely, but following these steps can help you turn water found in stale ponds, dirty creeks, or little puddles into water that's clean enough to drink. Without purifying the water, you risk becoming very sick, and no one wants that.

Using a Condensation System

A condensation system is an extremely easy way to get access to clean drinking water. However, it does require you to have one primary thing—a piece of plastic. It can be an old grocery bag, a sandwich bag, or even a piece of plastic wrap. In order to get the system to work, you will need to hang your piece of plastic somewhere, preferably on a shady tree branch. The bag will collect dew off the leaves and produce water inside of it due to the moisture in the air.

CHAPTER 10:

FORAGING

Although your body can go a long time without food, situations may require you to forage if you start feeling weak or sick. There are many things in the wilderness that are edible and don't require cooking at all. Most of the grass we walk on every day is edible. In this chapter, we will cover the many different types of edible berries, plants, mushrooms, morels, and even bugs. Depending on what part of the country you are in, the wilderness will often offer a large variety of food that you can eat. Food isn't quite as important as water, but foraging for food when you're lost is always a good thing. Sometimes, the weather may get too bad, and you won't be able to get out to forage. Having a stash of food nearby is important. Here are ways to forage in the wilderness and some examples of what you may find:

Why Foraging is Important

Finding food is very important for your health. While you are in the woods, you want to keep up your strength, and that means eating food. I know what you're thinking: vegetables, right? Yes, fruits and vegetables will be on the list of targets while you're foraging. But did you know that you can also eat certain kinds of bugs? You can also eat flowers and certain grasses as well. You have to be very careful, though. Some plants that look like they are supposed to be eaten are actually poisonous. Ask your parents or guardians to help you understand edible plants, or check out a book about foraging at the library for more information.

Vegetables you may find in the wild:

You may stumble across some wild vegetables growing in the wilderness, but be prepared — they may not look like what you see on the grocery store shelf. Wild-growing vegetables look more like weeds.

For example, did you know that dandelions are a vegetable? They are! They are incredibly nutritious as well. You can eat everything on a dandelion — the leaves, the stem, and the flower.

Nettles are another great and nutritious find. Nettles come in many different varieties. Some nettles sting, some smell funny, and some are very large. You will need to handle these carefully. Wrap something around your hand if you attempt to pick them. These should also not be eaten raw since they will hurt your mouth.

Purslane is yet another great find. Your parents or caregivers may hate finding purslane in the garden, but if you are in the wild and spot this plant, it is safe to eat and is very good for you.

Berries you may find in the wild:

Elderberry is a small purple berry found on bushes that have red stems. These berries taste great and are healthy for you.

Blackberries look very similar to raspberries. They grow on bushes and can be found all throughout the wild. The bushes don't typically grow very tall, and they're thick and covered with thorns. Be very careful when picking these berries.

Gooseberries, huckleberries, and mulberries are also great options. They are often only found during specific seasons.

Mushrooms you may find in the wild:

Mushrooms taste amazing and can help you keep up your energy if you're in the wild. However, it's very important to understand that some mushrooms can be extremely dangerous and will hurt you if you eat them. Find mushrooms that you can easily identify as edible. If you are unsure at all or don't remember if a mushroom is safe to eat, it's best not to risk it.

TYPES OF MUSHROOMS

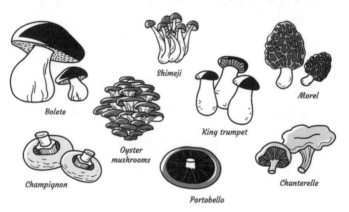

Bolete

Shimeji

Oyster mushrooms

King trumpet

Morel

Champignon

Portobello

Chanterelle

Lion's mane is easily identifiable since it has long white strands that resemble — you guessed it — a lion's mane. It is large and safe to eat.

Chanterelles are another form of edible mushroom that is commonly found throughout the United States.

Morels are unique and very easy to spot because of their honeycomb-like structure. They are edible and can help curb your hunger if you are in the woods for long periods of time.

Oyster mushrooms are found throughout the year all over the United States. They are pretty easy to spot and will usually be on the side of a decomposing tree trunk.

Nuts you may find in the wild:

Nuts are an excellent source of protein and vitamins. Many nuts can be found throughout wild environments. Pecans, acorns, walnuts and more can be found if you know what you're looking for.

Walnuts are amazing for you, but they can be tricky to spot if you're not sure what to look for. The surprising thing about most walnuts is that they are covered in a green, sometimes fuzzy outer layer. In order to get to the walnut inside, you have to tear off the outer layer. It may confusingly look like fruit at first.

Pecans grow from trees and are typically found in warmer climates. Wild pecans taste just like the kind you would find in the store, but the shells aren't as tough. They're easier to crack open and may even break during their growth cycle.

Acorns are one of the most common nuts found throughout North America. Acorns are common, and it's likely you can easily find some, but be warned — they taste awful raw. They are very bitter and will make your mouth pucker. If you have the resources and can boil them, they are much better. In an emergency, though, it's best to eat them however you can.

Bugs you can safely eat:

Gross! Bugs! Why would anyone eat bugs?! Well, if you are ever lost in the woods for a long time, bugs could be just the thing that prevents you from going hungry. It sounds super weird, but bugs have a lot of protein and honestly don't taste as bad as you might think.

Grasshoppers or crickets are some of the best bugs to eat. In other countries, people sometimes eat these little critters because of their high nutritional content. The only thing to keep in mind before you dine on one of these guys is that you should remove the legs and antennae to prevent choking.

Ants! Yep, ants. Usually, we hate ants getting near us while we are in the great outdoors. But if you're stuck out in the woods, ants may be just what you need. Ants taste sour if they are eaten raw but can prevent starvation. Keep in mind it will take a decent number of ants to keep you fed. Be sure to kill the ants before attempting to eat them; otherwise, you will have a sting or two on your tongue.

Ever seen *The Lion King*? Think like Timon and Pumba, and have yourself a grub. As gross as it sounds, grubs are high in vitamins and very helpful in keeping you healthy. Just look for a rotting log, tear it open, and *voila*! Dinner is served.

Earthworms are yet another slimy delicacy. If you find yourself in a rainy area, it's likely you'll encounter large amounts of earthworms. You can use this opportunity to gather as many as you'd like. However, these truly need to be cooked since they can carry parasites and other yucky things.

CHAPTER 11:

MAINTAINING OPTIMAL BODY TEMPERATURE

When out in the wilderness, protecting your health is important. So, one thing you should definitely understand for survival in the woods is how to keep your body working as it should. This is the reason finding a water source is so important. Water is the most effective way to stay healthy and energized when you are camping, hiking, or even lost in the woods. Staying hydrated is the most crucial thing when you are in the wilderness. It's also crucial to know how to keep your body temperature warm enough (and cool enough!) to prevent you from getting sick.

In this chapter, we will cover the dangers of heat exhaustion, dehydration, and hypothermia. You will also learn some ways to cool your body down if it gets too hot and how to warm up your body if the temperature drops too low.

Staying Cool

When in the wilderness, it's very important to maintain a cool body temperature when it's hot outside. It's easy to get overheated and dehydrated without noticing because you're so active. This can be very dangerous because if you wait too long to cool down your body, then you could become severely sick. If you don't keep your body cool while camping or hiking, this could also lead to injury from fatigue or exhaustion. Here are some ways to make sure your body stays cool while you're out in the woods:

WEAR PROTECTION

DON'T WEAR THICK CLOTHES

LIMIT OUTDOOR TIME

USE SUNSCREEN OR AN UMBRELLA

DRINK ENOUGH WATER

SHOWER IN COOL WATER

1. **Hydrate:** Let's say this word several times. Hydrate. HYDRATE! **HYDRATE! HYDRATE!** Drinking water is the absolute best way to stay healthy while in the woods. Water does several things for our body, and cooling it down is a very

important one. When our bodies get too hot, they start to release warmer water in the form of sweat. This water cools down your body when the air touches it. If you don't hydrate, your body won't be able to sweat enough, and your internal body temperature will get too hot.

2. **Light clothes:** It only makes sense, but if it's hot outside, you should be wearing short sleeves if possible. The clothes you wear should also fit loosely to allow good airflow. This will help keep your body cool and allow the air to touch your skin. Wearing materials like cotton is a good way to get the right airflow through your clothes so that your body doesn't overheat.

3. **Shade:** This one shouldn't be too hard to find while in the wilderness. Getting out of the sun will help keep your body cool. Find a large tree that provides a lot of shade and just relax under it as long as you need. Although the sun provides us with important vitamins, it can also be bad for your skin and your body temperature if you're exposed to it for too long.

4. **Water:** If you feel like you've gotten too hot, then in addition to drinking water, you can also use it to cool your body. If you have water to spare, gently pat your face with it. If you're near

a natural spring that's safe, you could even go soak in the spring to help you cool down.

5. **Wet cloth:** If you have an extra cloth, you can soak it in clean water and keep it on your head. This will serve as an "air conditioner" to keep your body temperature lower. When the wind blows, it will feel nice and cool.

Staying Warm

Now that you know how to keep your body cool, let's discuss staying warm. In the colder months, depending on where you are, cold weather can be very dangerous if you aren't prepared. If you're planning to go camping or hiking in late fall or the winter, you should definitely bring an emergency thermal blanket and warm clothes. A thermal blanket can be used not only for keeping you warm but also assist you when you need to build a shelter.

Warm clothes are clearly necessary to keep your body temperature up. Any time you are in the wilderness during colder months, you should pack extra clothes in case your clothes get wet due to the weather or falling in water or snow. If your body temperature gets too low, you are putting yourself at risk of getting sick. You could get hypothermia, which is a very dangerous situation that requires medical attention. Here are some ways to keep your body temperature higher in the cold:

1. **Warm clothes:** If you're in the wilderness during the winter, you should pack long-sleeved clothes, extra clothes, gloves, a thermal jacket, and a rain jacket. The best kind of clothes that you can wear to keep you warm will be made out of wool, silk, and a material like down. Down is made of bird feathers from geese or ducks.

2. **Thermal blanket:** If you're dressed warmly but still cold, then you can use the thermal blanket that you packed in your bag. A thermal blanket protects you from the elements, keeps you warm, and reduces your chances of getting hypothermia.

3. **Find cover:** So, you have dressed warmly and everything, but it's still way too cold outside! What else can you do? You should take shelter inside your tent or find a cover to block the wind. The wind can make a cool temperature seem like it's freezing, so it's very important that you find something to shield you from the

wind. This will help a lot in keeping your body temperature up.

4. **Build a fire:** If you use the survival skills mentioned earlier, you can stay by building a fire. The heat from your fire will keep you warm and help dry you and your clothes if you get wet.

5. **Eat:** Our bodies have to heat up in order to digest our food. If you eat a meal while you're cold, it will help you stay warmer.

How to Recognize Heat Exhaustion

Now that we've discussed how to stay cool, let's discuss what could happen if you don't keep your body cool while you're out having fun and exploring. Once your body gets too hot, it will start to overheat on the inside, and this can be very dangerous. It's extremely important that you try to avoid getting too hot because heat exhaustion is a much harder situation to deal with. The best way to avoid heat exhaustion is to drink plenty of water and take breaks. Here are ways to tell if you are experiencing heat exhaustion and what you should do if you are:

Heat Exhaustion Symptoms:

- **Cool and moist skin (even when in the heat)**
- **Headache**
- **Nausea**
- **Fast breathing**
- **Dizziness**
- **Feeling weak**
- **Swelling**
- **Bad (blurry) vision**

What should you do?

1. **Take a break:** As soon as you realize that you're getting too hot and have symptoms of heat exhaustion, you should immediately stop and take a break. Find good shade, sit down, and cool off.

2. **Soak your head:** Even if you seem to have chills, you should get a wet cloth and pat your head with it or set it on your neck.

3. **Create a breeze:** If you have your parents with you, they can help create a breeze by waving a branch with leaves. You can even do this yourself by taking a small stick with leaves on it to wave in front of your face while you're sitting down and cooling off.

4. **Drink water:** It's important to keep hydrating. It's very likely that you're dehydrated and that's

why you're experiencing heat exhaustion. So, take this time to slowly hydrate by drinking water and taking small sips.

5. **Emergency room:** If you're not feeling any better after a little while, you should have your parents or caregivers take you to the emergency room so that you can receive medical care.

How to Recognize Hypothermia

We've discussed how to stay warm, but you also need to know about hypothermia. Hypothermia is what happens to you when your body temperature drops too low. As discussed before, it's very important that you dress warmly and do what you can to avoid getting too cold. Sometimes, the weather may be colder than we expected, and we can't do anything about that. Next, you'll learn how to tell if you have hypothermia and what you should do if you have it.

Hypothermia Symptoms:
- **Difficulty remembering things**
- **Slow breathing**
- **Red skin**
- **Cold skin**

- **Mumbled speaking**
- **Uncontrollable shaking and shivering**
- **Difficulty thinking well**
- **Low energy**
- **Passing out**

What Should You Do?

The most dangerous thing about hypothermia is that you may not be able to tell if you have it. When you have hypothermia, you will likely be confused and have bad judgment. Therefore, it's clearly a bad situation and even worse if you're by yourself. If you think you may have hypothermia, the best thing you can do is find a way to warm up by getting to your shelter, putting on dry clothes if yours are wet, and sitting by a fire.

The best thing that can be done in this situation is have your parents get you to the hospital as soon as they can. They should help you get dressed in warm, dry clothes and find you place to warm up. You can even cuddle to use their body heat to warm you up. Most importantly, you need to get medical assistance from a doctor as soon as possible.

Remember that it's easy to forget about body temperature when you're out having fun. It's important to know ways to stay warm or cool in every type of weather. The best way to avoid a bad situation is to be careful and take care of yourself. The key things to remember are to hydrate, stay cool in hot weather, and stay warm in cold weather.

If you ever find yourself in a situation where you have gotten too hot or cold, you now have the skills to recognize heat exhaustion and hypothermia. You also have the skills to take care of yourself in this situation. HYDRATE!

CHAPTER 12:

BASIC FIRST AID AND HYGIENE

It goes without saying that the wilderness holds countless dangers. Some of these dangers may be things you hadn't even expected to happen during your camping or hiking trip. These can be as simple as infections, insect bites, or food poisoning, and the list goes on. With all the dangers in the woods, it's important to be prepared and know how to treat any sickness or wound you may get. All these possibilities make it very important for you to know survival skills that will help you take care of yourself if you're ever hurt. In this chapter, we will discuss how to recognize infections, take care of minor wounds, and care for any injuries you get while exploring outside.

Your health and safety is always the priority. When it comes to performing first aid on yourself, you should only do enough to keep you safe until you can get to a hospital or doctor. In this chapter, you'll learn basic skills that can prevent any infections or wounds from getting worse until you can be seen by a professional.

What to Do if Injured

Injuries are something that can happen anywhere at any time. When you're in the wilderness, injuries can be even more likely and more dangerous. Injuries are more dangerous while camping or hiking because resources are limited, and you're probably far away from any medical professionals. Sometimes, we do everything we can to be careful and not get hurt, but accidents still happen, and we get hurt anyway. In these situations, you have to relax and make sure you don't do anything to hurt yourself even worse. Next, we'll discuss different injuries that could happen while camping or hiking and how to tend to them.

Typical Injuries in the Woods

- **Broken or fractured bones:** These types of injuries can happen much easier than you'd think. You can break or fracture a bone just by landing on it the wrong way. A fracture or break of the bone is just as what it sounds like—your bone cracks or completely breaks in half, which will cause a lot of pain. You won't be able to move the broken bone or else it will hurt very badly. If the bone is broken or fractured, that part of your body will also swell.

- **Sprains:** Sprains are very common when hiking in the woods. A sprain is just an injury to the ligaments around the joints. A sprain isn't anything too severe, but you will experience a lot of swelling. Your sprain may also start to bruise around the joint.

- **Cuts:** Cuts can happen in many ways. You can be cut by tools, sticks, thorns, and many other things.

- **Impact Injuries:** Injuries to the head can easily happen from any fall. Any injury to the head should be treated very seriously because of how dangerous they are. Any time you hit your head on anything, you could experience many different types of injuries, which will be covered in this chapter.

- **Insect bites:** The wilderness has many different kinds of insects. Some of them are poisonous, some are harmless, and some can hurt you very badly if they sting or bite. Insect bites will usually cause rashes on the skin. If you are bitten by something poisonous, then it can cause bad swelling, bruising, and infections.

- **Animal bites:** There are many animals in the wilderness. Usually, animals will stay away from you, but it's always possible to get scratched or bitten. Bites can be minor, but many times, they can also be very dangerous. Animal bites can cause bleeding, swelling, bruising, and infections.

- **Skin irritation:** There are many things that grow in the woods. Some of these plants can irritate your skin. Poison ivy and poison oak can cause you to get a rash. If you're allergic, then this could be very dangerous.

How to Treat Injuries

1. **Broken or fractured bones:** If you ever break or fracture a bone, you need to find a way to rest it so that you don't make it worse. If your parents are with you, it's best that you tell them and have them help you.

   If the broken bone is causing bleeding, you should first tend to the bleeding. To do this, tie a knot above the break. Be careful, and don't tie the knot too tight. After you stop the bleeding, you need to completely cover the wound with some type of soft cloth or a bandage if you have a first aid kit with you.

If there is bleeding and you've already stopped it, you can now start creating a splint to hold the broken or fractured bone in place until you can get to a hospital. The reason you want to keep the bone in place is to reduce movement. If the bone moves too much, the break could get worse. Splinting the break will also reduce some of the pain.

To create the splint, you will just need at least two sticks, a long piece of cloth or bandage, and some type of padding to create a cushion. This cushion will help protect the injury from possible bumps that could happen while you're headed to the hospital.

Place a small stick on each side of the broken or fractured bone. While firmly holding the sticks in place, tightly wrap a bandage or cloth around the splints until the whole area is covered. Don't wrap it too tightly because that could cause your arm or leg to lose blood flow.

Now you need to create a cushion around the splint using extra cloth, bandages, and even hard materials like plastic if you have them. Things like duct tape can also be used as padding for the splint.

2. **Sprained joints:** Sprained joints aren't too serious, but they should still be treated carefully. The first thing you should do if you sprain a joint is get pressure off of it as soon as possible. After you get pressure off the sprain, carefully wrap the joint firmly but not too tightly. You can use bandages from your emergency kit, extra shirts, or socks. These will all be useful as wraps for your injury. After you have wrapped the joint, make sure you keep it elevated as much as possible.

3. **Cuts:** Cuts can vary in severity. How you begin to treat the cut will depend on how deep it is. If you have a minor cut, use clean water to wash the cut. If you have bandages, use them to cover the wound. If the cut is deeper and you find it difficult to get the bleeding to stop, you'll need to take more extensive measures. In the case of a deep cut, use a long strip of cloth or an extra shirt or jacket to create a tourniquet. Tie the material just above the cut in order to cut off blood flow. After that, use water to cleanse the

wound as best you can. Once clean, use strips of fabric to tie the wound closed and cover it.

4. **Impact Injuries:** If you find that you've fallen and don't know the severity of your head injury, take a moment to see how you feel. Do you feel dizzy? Nauseous? If so, then it's likely you have a concussion. You need to do what you can to stay awake, but don't overexert yourself. You need to be calm and rest your head, but sleeping is not a good idea for at least several hours. You should also inspect any bumps you may have on your head. If you feel a bump that is formed outward, then it is likely okay. However, if you find that you have a sunken-in area where you hit your head, that is extremely dangerous. You will need to find help as soon as possible. If you know that help can't be found quickly, try to find ways to keep yourself cool and rest.

5. **Insect bites:** While most insect bites are minor, some bites can cause severe rashes. In many cases, a severe rash can be helped by cleaning the area with soap. Make sure no stingers or insect parts are stuck inside the bite. Keep a cool, wet cloth on the bite for about 10 minutes.

6. **Animal bites:** First, clean the bite carefully with soap and water. After that, you need to stop any

bleeding. You can stop bleeding with gauze and bandages from your emergency kit. Once bleeding has stopped, you should use an antibiotic ointment on the bite. This will help prevent infection. If you start to notice more pain and strange colors on the bite after a few days, you should go to the doctor.

7. **Skin irritation:** Sometimes, we get too hot or may encounter bug bites or poisonous plants. Any of these issues can cause your skin to break out and make you feel uncomfortable. If you notice skin irritation, try to cleanse the area with cool water. If you have lotion or any other type of topical skin cream, it may help to put it over the area. If you have extra fabric like the ripped bottom of a shirt or jacket, cover the area to prevent further irritation.

CHAPTER 13:

WATER SAFETY AND FLOATING

Water safety is very important to your overall safety and well-being. Sometimes, we are very confident around water and feel like we can do anything. However, in a survival situation, you need to know what to do and what not to do in order to keep yourself safe. You might get the chance to go out on the lake with your family and splash around all day having fun. Maybe your parents or guardians even let you swim around without a life vest on. That is perfectly okay. The difference between that situation and a survival situation is that you can play all day and wear yourself out, knowing where you will sleep that night and that you'll be able to eat later. In a survival situation, you have to be careful and conserve your energy. You should also keep in mind that if you are hungry, you may not be able to swim as well as you normally would, meaning you may need to avoid getting in water that is above your head or does not allow your feet to touch the bottom.

Water Safety Rules in a Survival Situation

1. **Stay close to the shoreline:** Being in the water can offer you the opportunity to cool down and may provide some relief from soreness. But you need to remember that this isn't playtime. Don't go far from the shoreline.

2. **Don't wear your clothes in the water:** In a survival situation, you will want to keep the clothes you have dry. If you have spare clothes, you may use the opportunity to hand wash your shirts or underwear, but otherwise, don't get your clothes wet. You will need them to be dry once you leave the water.

3. **Don't swim near brush or trees:** These areas are notorious for snakes and other critters that can harm you.

4. **If you have an open wound, try not to put it in the water:** Lakes and ponds carry bacteria, and you don't know when you'll have proper access to wound care. Don't take the risk of getting your wound infected.

5. **Try to float -** Floating is an excellent way to allow your body to exert very little energy while still getting the benefits of the cool water.

If you don't have a lot of swimming experience and find yourself immersed in water, do what you can to flip onto your back with your face looking toward the sky. Do not panic. Take deep breaths in and out while focusing on keeping your chin up and your belly button up toward the sky. Once you begin floating, slowly move your arms up and down to move toward the shoreline or the water's edge. If that seems to be a long way off, navigate yourself to the nearest big rock or tree branch. Hold on to that rock and branch and take a minute to rest. Once you've had a break, calmly lay back in the water and begin floating again.

Water can be a great resource when treated carefully. In a survival situation, the last thing you want to do is forget that water can also be dangerous. Understand your limits so that you can keep yourself safe, not tire yourself out, and use the water for your benefit.

CONCLUSION

If used correctly, along with practice, this book can offer you great insight on how to protect yourself and stay safe in a variety of situations. Remember, the best way to be prepared in any situation is to know what to do before it happens. Get together with your parents or a close adult and create memories by safely practicing some of the scenarios in this book and planning out how you would handle each one. Remember, this must be done with an adult. While we all love to have fun with our friends, if something were to go wrong, an adult would be best suited to help you. Practicing and becoming a skilled survivalist will help you feel confident should danger ever come your way and will also be a skill set that will be helpful for the rest of your life. These may even become skills that you will one day teach to your children.

Remember, you are not be expected to be perfect when you begin practicing these skills. You can even turn some of the scenarios into fun games like a scavenger hunt for supplies. Have fun!